Ayo's Money Jar

By
Charlene Hill Fadirepo

CR Media, LLC 2016
SmartChoiceNation

Copyright 2016 ©
SmartChoiceNation
Trademark and copyright by
SmartChoiceNation, care of
CR Media, LLC.

All rights reserved. In accordance with the U.S. Copyright Act of 1976, the scanning, loading, and electronic sharing of any part of this book without the permission of the Publisher is unlawful piracy and the theft of this book's intellectual property. Thank you for your support of the author's rights.

This book series is dedicated to my father,
Charlie Wyatt Hill.

Daddy- Your daily "teachable moments", around the dinner table, taught me the importance of striving for long term financial independence. Hopefully this series can help teach the priceless lessons I learned from you.

Special Thanks to
Aniekan Udofia also known as
the "DC Muralist" for the book's
amazing Illustrations!

A Note to Parents,

Congratulations, you have taken the first step toward becoming a **financially empowered parent!** I hope this book helps you start a household conversation on financial education within your family.

Ayo's Money Jar is the first book in our series for children ages 2-6 called $mart¢hoiceNation (SCN) Kids. This is the second edition of the the Ayo's Money Jar book. This edition features beautiful original artwork from Nigerian visual artist, Aniekan Udofia. This version of the book also explores the multicultural heritage of the book's main character, Ayo.

Each SCN book is written as a conversation guide that covers a specific financial education concept. The conversation guide section includes suggested family activities and a glossary of terms to reinforce the learning process. Ayo's Money Jar focuses on money management, and explores the *Give, Grow, Go (3Gs)* concept, a SCN money management rule of thumb for children:

- *Give:* A portion of a child's allowance should be <u>shared</u> with those who are less fortunate.
- *Grow:* A portion of a child's allowance should be <u>saved</u>, so that it can grow or increase over time.
- *Go:* A portion of a child's allowance should be <u>spent</u> on or go toward those items that a child desires.

Money decisions drive hopes, dreams, life goals and aspirations. By teaching your children these concepts today, you will help secure the economic future of your family now and for generations to come.

Sincerely,
Charlene Hill Fadirepo
Founder of SmartChoiceNation

Key Questions To Ask After the Story!
1) What are the 3 Gs?
2) Why is important to give?
3) How did Ayo make his money grow?
4) What did Ayo receive from his Mama and Daddy after he did his chores?
5) What did Ayo spend his money on?

Check us out online at www.smartchoicenation.com
Twitter: @SmartCNation

2 little quarters in my Money Jar,
2 little quarters don't go very far.
Mama told me a secret,
that many don't know.
If I save them up, my
quarters will Grow!

3 little quarters in my Money Jar,
3 little quarters don't go very far.
Mama told me a secret that many don't know,
If I work really hard my quarters will Grow.

Hurray, Mama gave me a quarter for sweeping the kitchen floor!

4 little quarters in my Money Jar,
4 little quarters might go pretty far.
4 little quarters make my money jar sing,
It sounds like ting-a-ling-a-ling!

Grandmama stopped by and gave me a quarter for helping her with her bags!

5 little quarters in my Money Jar, 5 little quarters should go really far.

Mama says tomorrow we will go to the store, where they have ice cream, treats and so much more!

We went to the store and I used 3 quarters to Go toward an ice cream cone for my big sister and I.

I even had 2 quarters left over!

I decided to Give one quarter to the man sitting outside the store.
I saved my last quarter, so it could Grow in my Money Jar.

1 little quarter saved in my Money Jar,
1 little quarter won't go very far.
Spent 3 quarters on treats, and gave one away;
I followed the Give, Grow, Go rule all in one day !!!

The Give Go Grow Rule can be followed every day, the money you earn can be used in three ways.

The rule is so simple and easy to do, to make sure you remember, LET'S REVIEW!!

An <u>allowance</u> is money earned for <u>chores</u>, like carrying Grandmama's bags or sweeping the floor,

Or making the bed or cleaning the table,
Helping your parents is good, do as much as you're able.

A quarter is the same as 25 pennies,
Piggy banks should be chubby and never skinny,

But you can't see through them, so they are not up to par,
To really grow your money use a Money Jar!

Key Money Management Terms

1. **Allowance:** money earned by a child as a result of the completion of weekly chores or other assigned work.

2. **Chore:** a job or activity assigned by your Mama or Daddy.
   Example: In the story, Ayo earned his allowance by completing his chores which were to make the bed and sweep the floor.

3. **Give:** A portion of a child's allowance should be shared with those who may be in need. *(SmartChoiceNation Money management rule of thumb)*

4. **Grow:** A portion of a child allowance should be saved, so that it can grow or increase over time. *(SmartChoiceNation Money management rule of thumb)*

5. **Go:** A portion of a child's allowance should be spent on or go toward those items that a child wants. *(SmartChoiceNation Money management rule of thumb)*

6. **Needs:** Basic items required for someone's health, education, and general well being.
   Example: In the story, Ayo gave one quarter to the man sitting outside of the door. This man will most likely use this money for food, which is a basic need. Other needs are a safe place to live, and clothing.

Key Money Management Terms

7. **Save:** To put aside money for future use.
   Example: In the story, Ayo saved one of his quarters for later, after he had given one away and spent three on ice cream.

8. **Wants:** Extra special items that a child may desire, but does not need. Items that a child wants should be provided by parents, but only on a limited basis. Consider encouraging your child to save his/her allowance to pay for portions of the cost of their "want" items. This will help reinforce the concept that "want" items are extra special and might require a level of sacrifice. Two simple examples of age appropriate sacrifice would be to: 1) delay the purchase of a want item for a period of time or 2) ask the child to give up an older used toy in exchange for the new want item. These steps will help your child develop the critical concept of gratitude and compassion for others in need.
   Example: In the story, Ayo wanted ice cream and other treats, yet these items were not absolutely necessary for his health.

MONEY MANAGEMENT QUESTIONS ONLY

GIVE, GO, GROW

What are the 3 Gs?

Why is it important to Give?

How did Ayo make his money Grow?

What did Ayo's quarters Go toward?

MONEY JAR

Where did Ayo store his money?

Can you think of other places to store money?

Why do we store money in special places?

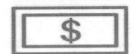

ALLOWANCE/EARNING

What did Ayo receive from Mama and Daddy after he did his chores?

How can you earn an allowance?

MONEY MANAGEMENT QUESTIONS & ANSWERS

GIVE, GO, GROW

What are the 3 Gs?
(Give, Grow, Go)

Why is it important to Give?
(Giving allows us to show love and support for those in need.)

How did Ayo make his money Grow?
(Ayo made his money grow by saving it in his Money Jar.)

What did Ayo's quarters Go toward?
(Hint: It was for yummy want, not a need. Ayo used his money to buy ice cream, a very yummy want indeed.)

MONEY JAR

Where did Ayo store his money?
(In his Money Jar!)

Can you think of other places to store money?
(In a bank or your wallet.)

Why do we store money in special places?
(We store money in special places to keep it safe.)

ALLOWANCE/EARNING

What did Ayo receive from Mama and Daddy after he did his chores?
(Hint: One chore was to sweep the floor. Ayo received one quarter after every chore he completed.)

How can you earn an allowance?
(An allowance can be earned by helping Mama and Daddy around the house. A few ideas are picking up your toys, turning off the lights, and making your bed.)

LEARN MORE ABOUT AYO & HIS FAMILY

Map of the United States

AYO'S FAMILY

Ayo comes from a multicultural family -- his Mama is African American from the United States and his Daddy is from Ibadan, Nigeria.

Where are your parents from?

LANGUAGES SPOKEN IN AYO'S HOME

There are 2 languages spoken in Ayo's home, English and Yoruba.

Ayo's Mama speaks English. Ayo's Daddy speaks Yoruba. Yoruba is a language spoken in West Africa, mainly in Nigeria. Yoruba is also the name of one of the largest ethnic groups in Nigeria.

What languages are spoken in your home?

Map of Africa

WHAT'S IN A NAME?

Naming traditions for children typically vary across cultures.

Ayo's full first name is Ayodele. Ayodele means "Joy comes into this house" in Yoruba.

What does your name mean?

Were you named after someone special in your family?

Money Management
Family Activity #1
Do-It-Yourself Money Jars

Objective	Supplies Needed	Activity Costs	Notes
• Encourage good money habits by creating money jars for your kids to use. • Put the Give, Grow, Go rule into practice!	• 3 clear plastic jars (with screw on tops) • Several small colorful stickers • Markers • Clear tape • Blank sticky address labels or small pieces of paper the size of Post-It Notes	• Minimal • Cut costs by reusing old mayonnaise containers	• Activity is great for older kids as well! • You will need 3 containers per child • Bonus: Once the jar is half full, create a guessing game to guess the amount of money in the jar.

Activity Time: 30 Minutes
Activity Complexity: Easy

Before you start:
- Make sure the plastic jars are clean, if you are reusing old ones.
- There are two options for getting money into the jar. Option 1 requires an adult to cut a slit in the plastic top of the jar. Option 2 is to simply use the screw on/off feature of the jar to add money to it.

Instructions:
1. Write the words GIVE, on one of the sticky labels. Let your child tape the GIVE label to middle of the jar's base. Create GO and GROW labels and affix them to each of the other jars.
2. Let your child use different stickers to decorate the jars. Be sure not to use too many stickers ---the great thing about a money jar is that you can actually see how much money is in there!
3. Establish a saving schedule for your child. Encourage your child to add money to the jars at least once a week.
4. Help build up the balance in your child's jars by adding loose pocket change from time to time. Once the jar is at least half full, travel to a coin counter machine and see how much your child's money has grown!

Money Management
Family Activity #2
Wants vs Needs Vision Boards

Objective	Supplies Needed	Activity Costs	Notes
• Gain a better understanding of wants vs. needs. • Identify specific examples of wants and needs. • Establish the link between wants and the importance of saving for extra special items.	• Poster board • Stacks of old magazines • Child safety scissors • Glue Stick • Large markers	• Minimal • Cut costs by reusing old magazines	• Try the high tech version of the activity for older kids. Use Pinterest to create Wants/Needs vision board online. (Supervise the child's use of the internet.)

Activity Time: 45 Minutes
Activity Complexity: Medium

Before you start:
- Make sure you have pulled together a variety of magazines with plenty of photos.
- Review the definitions of wants vs needs from the Money Management Term Glossary.
- Brainstorm examples of wants vs needs that might appear in magazines. For example a want might be appear in an advertisement for a luxury watch or fancy car. A need might appear in advertisement for food.

Instructions:
1. Use the marker to draw a line and divide the vision poster board into two sections.
2. Write WANTS at the top of the first section and NEEDS at the top of the second section of the vision board.
3. Let your child cut pictures of wants and needs out of the magazines and glue the pictures to the appropriate side of the board.
4. Once complete, discuss the vision board with your child. Be sure to point out examples of extra special items that might require saving as well as extra sacrificed prior to purchasing.
5. Encourage your child to make a list of their wants. Hold on to that list so that these items can be purchased over time once the appropriate amount of money has been saved.

Money Management
Family Activity #3
Charitable Giving

Objective	Supplies Needed	Activity Costs	Notes
• Encourage your child to develop a giving heart by experiencing the act of giving.	• At least $1-2 dollars (in coins) available to give away • A few additional dollars in order to match your child's gift.	• Gas for travel to giving location	• Activity works best for kids 4+. • Activity can be repeated weekly!

Activity Time: 30 Minutes – 1 Hour (based on travel time)
Activity Complexity: Medium

Before you start:
- This activity works well, once the child has saved at least 1 to 2 dollars (in coins) of his/her own money. If you have completed Activity #1, and there are coins in the GIVE jar, start by counting the number of coins and money amount in the jar.
- Identify 2-3 places where your child can experience "the act of giving". Suggested examples include: church offering plate, charity organizations within grocery stores—especially those that allow your family to post an in-store notice of your gift. The Salvation Army bucket during the holidays is also a great source of giving.
- Review the definitions of wants vs needs from the Money Management Term Glossary.

Instructions:
1. Discuss the section of the story where little Ayo was able to give a portion of his savings to the man outside of the store. Discuss why giving is important.
2. Count the amount of savings out loud with your child and work together to decide on an amount to set aside to give away. 10% of the savings amount is recommended. (For example if your child has $1.00, plan to give away 10 cents).
3. Allow your child to experience "the act of giving". Let him/her place the gift in the offering plate, or hand the money to the cashier. Discuss the importance of giving and if possible –match your child's gift with your own funds.
4. Establish a giving schedule for your child –and stick to it! Make giving a regular money habit for your child.

About the Author: Charlene Fadirepo

Charlene Hill Fadirepo is a former banker, financial educator, author and speaker with more than 15 years of experience in financial services. Charlene also is the founder of SmartChoiceNation (SCN), a social enterprise financial education company dedicated to empowering America's youth-- especially girls, to make smarter financial and life skills choices. She currently serves as the President of Greater Washington Jumpstart Coalition, a youth focused financial literacy organization within the DC metro area. Charlene is a former Math and Science teacher via the Higher Achievement Program in Baltimore, and she works as an advocate for financial literacy in the DC metro area. Before founding SCN, Charlene was a management consultant within the financial services industry.

Charlene obtained her Masters in Business Administration (MBA), from the Fuqua School of Business at Duke University and studied Electrical Engineering at the University of Virginia. She lives in Washington, DC with her husband, Rinde and 3 year old son, Ayodele. She also runs a blog called SmartChoiceMoms.com, which celebrates financially empowered parenthood.

Learn more about SCN here - www.smartchoicenation.com
www.smartchoicemoms.com

About the Illustrator: Aniekan Udofia

Aniekan Udofia has established a formidable reputation as a powerful painter and illustrator. Whether through multi-layered compositional complexity, suggestive narrative or straightforward human form, in his work, there is often autobiographical narrative at play.
The 36 year old Udofia has achieved DC notoriety for his majestic towering murals of Duke Ellington and Fredrick Douglas as well as his solo and group live paintings at Washington events. He has a solid clientele list including Red Bull, Heineken, Honda, Timberland and Adidas, Toyota, American Express, The Office of Unified communications, Murals DC, Museum of Public Art and a host of small businesses and property owners.

Udofia garnered national attention in the early 2000s with his illustrations working for publications such as XXL, Vibe, DC Pulse, Frank151, While you where Sleeping and The Source. His murals share the rich vibrant history and culture of the different communities they are created in. Whether it's the gagged George Washington on 15th and U street or the very bright and colorful Marvin Gaye in the Shaw area of Washington, DC, Udofia's public works speak for themselves. Aniekan lives and works in his studio in the Adams Morgan area of Washington, DC.

Check Aniekan out online at aniekanudofia.com

$mart¢hoiceNation

Book #1 of the $mart¢hoiceNation Kids Series: Money Management

Ayodele (Ayo) is a curious little boy growing up in a multicultural family. When Ayo helps his Mama and Daddy around the house, he gains way more than he bargained for and learns a lasting lesson about money management.

Get all of the books in the series for children ages 2-6 !!

Did you like this book? Let us know:
www.smartchoicenation.com
Twitter: @SmartCNation
information@smartchoicenation.com
Facebook:
http://www.facebook.com/smartchoicenation

Made in the USA
Middletown, DE
13 October 2016